Insect Maths

Insect Maths

Rachael Davis

Collins

Contents

CHAPTER 1:
The world of insects

Mighty maths

Insects use lots of different maths tricks to help them survive in the wild. Some insects use patterns on their body to attract a mate. Other insects use patterns to disguise themselves and keep **predators** away. Even an insect's body is mathematical!

There are millions of different insects with unique bodies. But there is one maths fact that is shared by all insects …

All insects have three pairs of legs! That's six legs in total.

The body of an insect is made up of three parts called the head, thorax and abdomen.

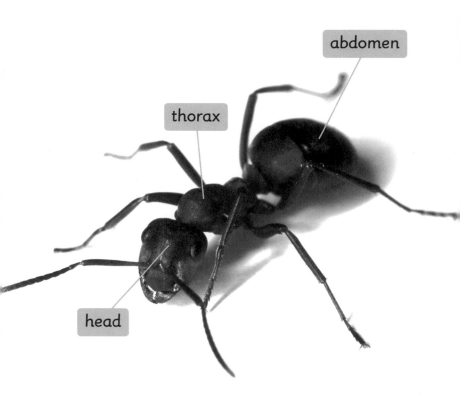

abdomen

thorax

head

DID YOU KNOW?

An insect's skeleton is on
the outside of its body.
It is called an **exoskeleton**.

3

Extraordinary eyes

Many insects have compound eyes.
Compound eyes are made up of
mini hexagonal-shaped **lenses**.
There can be over 1,000 of these
lenses in an insect's eye.

WHAT DO INSECTS SEE?

The lenses in an insect's compound eye mean
that insects see differently from humans.
Each hexagonal part of the insect's eye
shows a mini-section of the thing the insect is
looking at. This means that what insects see
is blurrier than what humans see.

MATHS IN ACTION!

Hexagons can form a tessellation.
A tessellation is a repeated pattern of shapes
which can fit together without any gaps
or overlapping.

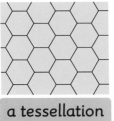

a tessellation
of hexagons

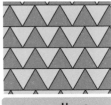

a tessellation
of triangles

Not all shapes can form tessellations.
When you put some shapes side by side,
there are gaps between them.

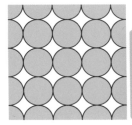

Circles can't form
a tessellation because
there are always gaps
between them.

How insects are grouped

Scientists divide animals into groups based on their similarities and differences. They have divided insects into lots of different groups. Here are some of the main ones.

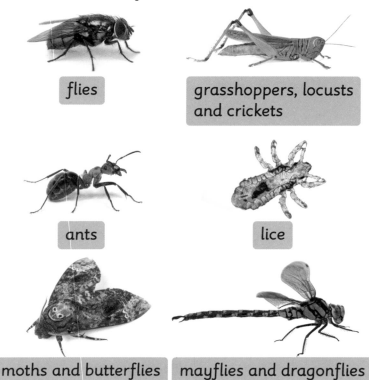

flies

grasshoppers, locusts and crickets

ants

lice

moths and butterflies

mayflies and dragonflies

Some groups of insects can fly, but others cannot. Flying insects often have four wings. But some flying insects have two soft wings and two hard wings. The hard wings act as a shell.

true bugs

beetles

praying mantises

cockroaches and termites

stick insects and leaf insects

earwigs

Insect impostors!

Some animals are mistaken for insects, but their number of legs shows they are not.

A spider is NOT an insect, because it has eight legs. In fact, a spider is more like a scorpion than an insect! This is because a spider and a scorpion are both arachnids.

Arachnids are the most common group of animals that are mistaken for insects. Although arachnids have lots in common with insects, they have lots of differences too.

Can you distinguish between insects
and arachnids?

	insects	arachnids
number of legs	six	eight
number of body parts	three	two
exoskeleton	yes	yes

It is not only arachnids that get mistaken
for insects. This happens to other kinds of
animals, too like the centipede and the millipede.

People often think that centipedes must have
100 legs because the "cent" bit in their
name means 100. In fact,
they can have between
30 and 354 legs!

A millipede has a lot more than six legs, and
sometimes even more than 1,000 legs!

Remarkable records!

There are millions of kinds of insects and some are mathematical record breakers!

Highest jumper

Froghoppers are small insects, about half a centimetre long. But they can jump up to 70 centimetres high! This is the same as a three-year-old child jumping over the London Eye!

Smallest insect

The tiniest insects are featherwing beetles, which are only a quarter of a millimetre in length. A line of 40 featherwing beetles would be I centimetre long!

Longest insect

The longest insect found so far is a stick insect that was 64 centimetres long.

Heaviest insect

Goliath beetles are the heaviest insects, weighing up to 100 grams. That's about the same as an apple!

Loudest insect

The African cicada's song is almost 107 **decibels**. That's as noisy as a chainsaw!

Tallest insect nest

Termites build the highest nests. Termite nests 12 metres high (about the height of three double-decker buses) have been found in Africa!

Largest swarm

Locusts travel in the largest swarms. A swarm of over 12 trillion locusts was found in America!

Fastest flyer

Dragonflies are the fastest flying insects. Some can fly up to 58 kilometres per hour!

Insect record holder map

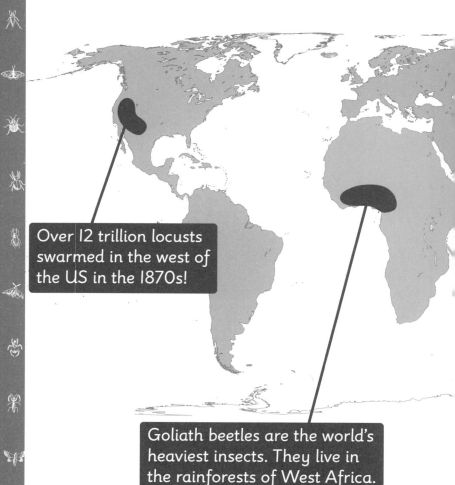

Over 12 trillion locusts swarmed in the west of the US in the 1870s!

Goliath beetles are the world's heaviest insects. They live in the rainforests of West Africa.

The longest insects in the world are stick insects. The longest one ever was found in south China!

Australian dragonflies are the fastest flying insect ever recorded!

African cicadas are the loudest insects. They are found all over Africa.

13

CHAPTER 2:
Incredible wings

Mathematical patterns

Lots of insects have wings, but the shape and pattern of their wings can vary. Most insects have two pairs of wings – forewings at the top and hindwings at the bottom. Their wings have a pattern of tiny veins. This pattern is unique to each kind of insect.

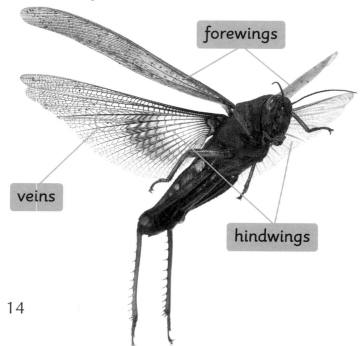

forewings

veins

hindwings

DID YOU KNOW?

Scientists hope they can learn from the earwig's superior folding techniques to pack large objects into small spaces. This would be very helpful to astronauts travelling into space because they can fit more equipment into their space rockets!

Amazing moths

Not all moths have beige wings!

Look at these amazingly colourful moths.

The rosy maple moth feeds mostly on maple trees.

The hummingbird moth flaps its wings so fast it can hover. Its wings are see-through.

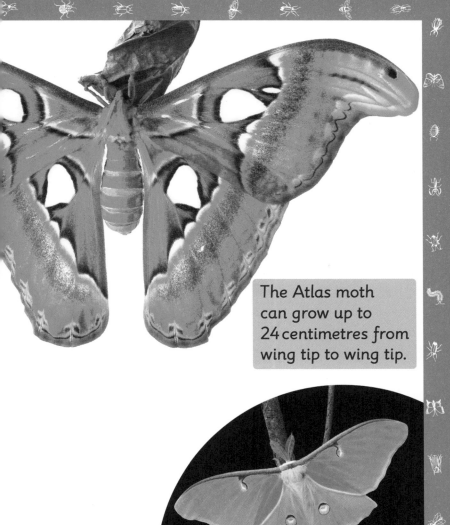

The Atlas moth can grow up to 24 centimetres from wing tip to wing tip.

The luna moth has no mouth and does not eat anything!

CHAPTER 3:
From egg to butterfly

Life cycles

There are four stages in the life cycle of a butterfly.

The process of a caterpillar turning into a butterfly is called metamorphosis. It takes place inside the pupa which protects the caterpillar while it transforms.

Caterpillars are insects too. Just like the butterflies they transform into, caterpillars have three pairs of legs. However, they also have up to five pairs of **prolegs** that help them move across leaves.

legs

prolegs

The life cycle of a butterfly

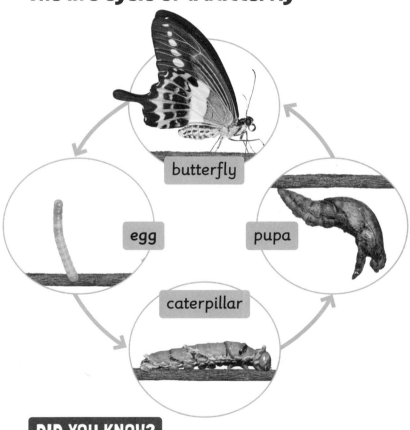

butterfly

egg

pupa

caterpillar

DID YOU KNOW?

All butterflies and moths go through this life cycle!

Butterfly symmetry

Butterflies' bodies are mathematical because ...
they are symmetrical! An object is symmetrical
if it is the same on both sides. If you draw a line
down the middle of a butterfly's body, the pattern
on its wings is the same on both sides.

Butterflies have symmetrical patterns on their
wings – but these are not just beautiful to
look at! They also help the butterflies to survive.
Butterflies use their wings to camouflage and
disguise themselves from predators.

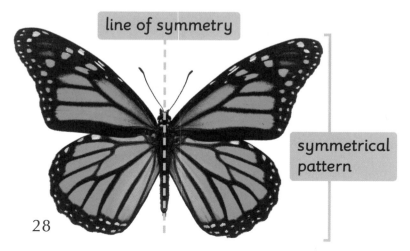

line of symmetry

symmetrical
pattern

FLOWER POWER!

Symmetrical wings are not the only place butterflies use mathematical patterns to help them survive. They also see patterns in flowers which humans cannot see! Butterflies can see more colours than humans can. The extra colours make flowers look more patterned to butterflies than they do to humans.

how a human sees a flower

how a butterfly sees the same flower

Disguised to survive

Some butterflies use **mimicry** to deceive predators. They disguise themselves by mimicking the way another animal looks!

The symmetry in butterflies' wings gives them a unique advantage. Some butterflies **mimic** other animals' eyes on their wings. This amazing wing pattern is called eyespots.

Predators often mistake the two eyespots for the face of a larger predator. This scares them away.

Some butterflies have more than one pair of eyespots, making them even more confusing for predators.

Butterflies have adapted to use mimicry in different ways.

Hairstreak butterflies are plain apart from their wing tips, which mimic a more traditional butterfly pattern. If a predator eats the wing tip, thinking it's a whole butterfly, the butterfly can still survive!

The owl butterfly not only has eyespots but its wing patterns even look like an owl's face!

Mimicry is also used at other times in the butterfly life cycle. The giant swallowtail caterpillar disguises itself by mimicking bird poo!

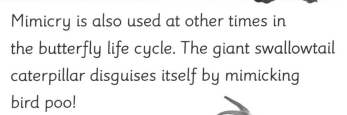

The brightest blue

One of the brightest-coloured butterflies in the world is the blue morpho butterfly. It uses the science of how light travels to create its colourful wings.

The blue morpho butterfly's wings are made up of tiny scales that act like mini prisms. When sunlight reaches the morpho butterfly's wings, the light that reflects back is blue.

blue morpho butterfly

scales

MATHS IN ACTION!

White light is made up of seven colours. We see these in a rainbow. When waves of white light travel through a prism, it bends and splits into its seven colours.

prism

When light splits, the blue light travels slowly and spreads out more than the other colours of light. Our eyes see more blue light than any other colour. This is why the blue morpho butterfly's wings appear blue.

DID YOU KNOW?

It can be hard to tell butterflies and moths apart. People often say that butterflies have bright wings and moths have beige wings. But in fact, some butterflies are beige and many moths are brightly coloured!

Impressive migration

Some butterflies migrate. This means they travel when the seasons change, to find food and survive. They might migrate thousands of kilometres to do this. They follow the same migration pattern every year.

The painted lady butterfly migrates to Africa every autumn!

Millions of monarch butterflies travel over 4,800 kilometres from the US to Mexico every autumn.

Butterflies fly in different ways. It depends on how many times they flap their wings per second.

Gliding – the biggest butterflies tend to glide and don't flap their wings very often at all.

Flapping – the most common kind of flight involves butterlies flapping their wings between five and twenty times per second.

Butterflies called skippers are the fastest flyers. They can fly at speeds of up to 59 kilometres per hour!

Caterpillar patterns!

Some caterpillars have brightly-patterned bodies to warn off predators, or to act as a disguise or camouflage.

WARNING!

Bright colours warn predators that the caterpillar might be poisonous or taste unpleasant.

CAMOUFLAGE

Some caterpillars use camouflage to blend in with their surroundings. Some look like twigs or bird droppings.

DISGUISE!

False eyespots distract predators, or mimic snakes to scare predators away!

CHAPTER 4:
Warning stripes

Stripes are among the most common patterns found on insects' bodies. Bees, wasps and hornets have developed black and yellow stripes to warn predators that they can sting. Predators quickly learn to avoid flying insects with yellow and black stripes, and this helps stripy insects to survive.

Hornets are a kind of wasp, but they have wider heads and rounder bodies than other wasps. Wasps and hornets have skinny hairless bodies. Bees tend to have wide, hairy bodies.

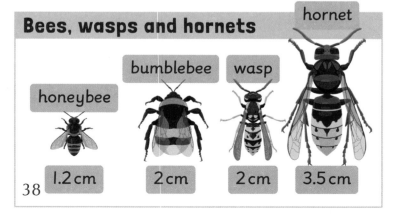

Bees, wasps and hornets

hornet

bumblebee

wasp

honeybee

1.2 cm

2 cm

2 cm

3.5 cm

Deceptive disguises

The hornet moth uses mimicry to deceive predators. It looks just like a hornet! Predators know that hornets can sting them. So they are more likely to stay away from the harmless moth, thinking they might get stung.

Would you believe this is a hornet moth, and not an actual hornet?

Honeycombs

Honeybees use maths techniques to store
the largest amount of honey possible.
They store their honey in **honeycombs** which
are made up of hexagonal-shaped wax cells.
They use this tessellating design because
the repeating pattern has no gaps, and
the structure is very strong.

DID YOU KNOW?

Honeybees are not the only insects that
create hexagonal tessellations. Paper wasps
do this as well, when building their nest.
The queen builds hexagonal
cells for her eggs.

Why do bees make hexagonal honeycombs?

When bees make honeycombs, they start with a wax circle. Then they use their body heat to melt the wax and turn the circle into a hexagon.

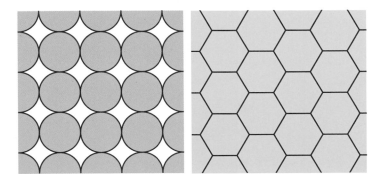

But why do bees choose hexagons? Squares or triangles would tesselate too. Well, bees are very clever engineers. They have worked out that the hexagon uses the least amount of wax to hold the most weight! This means that their honeycombs can hold more honey and store it safely.

Dancing bees

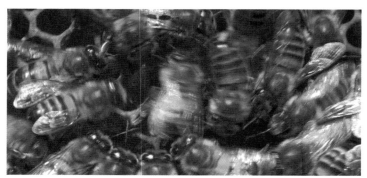

Scientists have discovered that honeybees
have a unique language ... dancing!
When a honeybee returns to the hive carrying
food, it can remember where it found the food.
Through a rhythmic waggling dance, it can tell
other honeybees the exact position of the food.

the honeybee
"waggle" dance

MATHS IN ACTION!

We use maths to work out the distance and direction needed to get from one place to another (from place A to place B).

A honeybee uses the same maths to remember where food is! The waggle dance tells other honeybees about the direction and distance to food so that they can find the food too.

CLEVER COUNTING

It seems that bees can count up to five! In 2022, a team of scientists conducted an **experiment** to find out if bees can count. The results were astonishing! The scientists showed that bees can identify and order numbers from one to five.

Parasites!

Parasitic wasps are a kind of **parasite** that live inside another insect. They lay their eggs inside the eggs or pupa of butterflies and moths. The baby wasps hatch and eat the caterpillar. Later, a fully-grown wasp comes out of the pupa instead of a butterfly!

MATHS IN ACTION!

Parasitic wasps are not all bad.

When an unwanted insect or pest is eating farmers' crops, we need to find ways to quickly lower the number of pests. Scientists studying parasitic wasps have learned some great new ideas for getting rid of pests.

Wasp shock

One of the first people to discover parasitic wasps was a scientist called Maria Merian. Maria was born nearly 400 years ago. She started collecting insects as a teenager. She recorded her findings in books and drew pictures of them. Maria was shocked when one day she was drawing a butterfly's pupa and a wasp came out of it!

Maria's picture of the butterfly's life cycle

Maria Merian

Patterns for protection

Most kinds of insects lay eggs. Eggs can be an easy target for hungry predators or parasitic wasps. Some insects use patterns to disguise their eggs from predators. Some insect eggs have patterns that make them look dangerous or poisonous! This dissuades predators from getting too close.

The patterns are unique to the various kinds of insect. They can be stripy, spotty, multicoloured or even … frilly!

MATHS IN ACTION!

Bees and wasps are not the only insects that use hexagons. Some insects lay eggs in a hexagonal shape on leaves!

This shield bug lays its eggs close together in a hexagonal pattern.

Beware the zombie wasp

This emerald jewel wasp depends on cockroaches for survival.

First, it stings the cockroach which paralyses it. Then it stings the cockroach's brain.

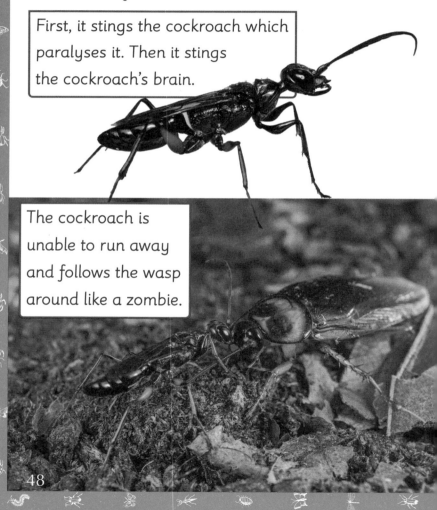

The cockroach is unable to run away and follows the wasp around like a zombie.

The wasp lays its eggs on the cockroach.
The grub hatches and feeds on the cockroach.

The grub transforms into a wasp.
It bursts out of the cockroach.

CHAPTER 5:
Millions of beetles!

Beetles come in a variety of different colours, shapes and sizes. Most beetles have horns and powerful jaws. However, they look and behave very differently!

Featherwing beetles are one of the smallest ...

... while Goliath beetles are the biggest and heaviest.

Titan beetles are the longest.

DID YOU KNOW?

There are around one million different kinds of insects in the world and nearly half of them are some kind of beetle.

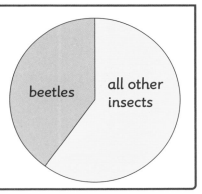

beetles

all other insects

Some beetles, like fireflies, can glow ...

... while others are multicoloured and even shimmer!

This Australian pie dish beetle hides by disguising itself as a seed! If it is under attack, it tilts its wide, flat body at an angle to defend itself.

Ladybirds

There are around 5,000 different kinds of ladybirds in the world. Often ladybirds have a red exterior with black spots. The ladybird's bright colour and spots are a warning to predators that they taste bad or are even poisonous! Scientists have shown that the redder the ladybird, the more deadly it is to predators. The pattern and number of spots varies for different kinds of ladybirds.

A common kind is the seven-spotted ladybird.

DID YOU KNOW?

Some people think the number of spots tells you a ladybird's age, but that is not true!

Ladybirds have hardened forewings.

Their hindwings are beneath the forewings.

These are folded up just like earwig wings!

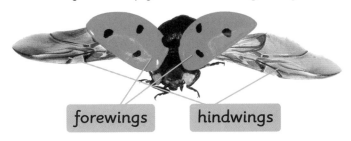

forewings   hindwings

The forewings are usually red. However, not all ladybirds have a red exterior.

Some have a yellow body with black spots ...

... while others have a black body with red spots!

DID YOU KNOW?

The pattern on a ladybird's forewings is symmetrical. They have the same pattern on each wing, a bit like a butterfly.

Spraying beetles

Bombardier beetles use **complex** maths and science to scare off predators. They spurt out boiling hot liquid from their abdomen which makes a loud POP! Not only are they fast but they can hit a predator from far away. This can save the bombardier beetle's life!

The bombardier beetle has an ingenious and unique abdomen. Inside it, there is a one-millimetre space where chemicals mix together and get very hot. This happens very quickly, whenever the beetle needs to defend itself from a predator. The chemical mixture is a good weapon! The beetle sprays this burning liquid at lightning speed over predators. The beetle can spray the liquid a distance of 20 centimetres. That's 200 times the length of its abdomen chamber!

MATHS IN ACTION!

Inventors have copied bombardier beetles to develop new fire extinguishers! The new fire extinguishers have a space inside, like the chamber inside the beetle.

 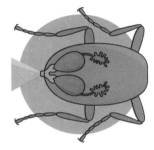

Using the new extinguishers, firefighters can spray water on fires from much further away than they could before. So they can extinguish a fire safely, if it is too dangerous to get close.

Creative colours

Some animals have shimmering, multicoloured bodies. This kind of colour is called iridescence. The jewel beetle has an iridescent body which helps it survive.

MATHS IN ACTION!

An iridescent animal looks a different colour depending on where you see it. This is because the colours of light bounce off the animal in all different directions. It can look as if the colours are changing or getting brighter.

In 2020, scientists discovered that jewel beetles use their iridescence to disguise themselves. The scientists put various coloured beetles on leaves and studied which ones were found by predators. The beetles with iridescent bodies were harder for predators to find.

DID YOU KNOW?

The original meaning of the word *iridescence* is "rainbow-coloured".

Walking on water!

Some insects can walk on water! When most objects hit water, they sink. But some insects have legs that **repel** water. Their legs and the water surface push against each other. This allows them to walk on water.

Water striders skate across one metre of water per second!

MATHS IN ACTION!

Scientists are using these water-repelling insects as inspiration to create water-walking robots!

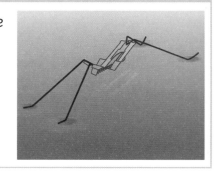

58

Lilypad beetles have an even more unique technique. Their legs are covered in tiny hairs that repel water, but the claws at the tip of their legs are hairless. This allows them to lock their claws onto the water. They flap their wings so they zoom across the water surface as if they are windsurfing!

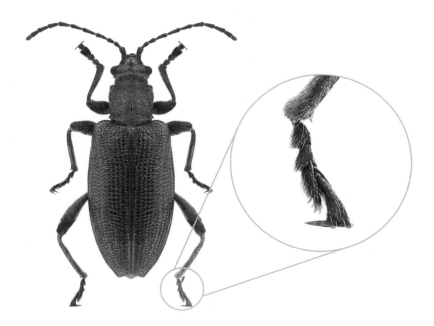

CHAPTER 6:
What a noise!

Some insects are noisy because it helps them to warn off predators. Others make a noise to attract a mate. But did you know there are lots of different ways that insects can make noises? For example, bees and wasps buzz by flapping their wings. Some bees can flap their wings 230 times a second! The flapping makes the buzzing noise.

Bombardier beetles make a loud popping sound when they spray hot liquid. However, the most common way for insects to make a noise is by rubbing two body parts together. Grasshoppers make noise by rubbing their back legs against their wings. Crickets make noise by rubbing their wings together. Some cicadas have a unique abdomen that makes a clicking sound.

Insect music

Crickets use musical patterns to attract a mate. Each kind of cricket creates its own unique rhythm. This allows female crickets to identify the right mate.

The pitch of a tree cricket's song changes with the temperature. When the weather is warmer, tree crickets chirp more quickly, and they also chirp with a higher pitch.

Tunnel tunes

One of the loudest insects in the world is the mole cricket. The sound a mole cricket makes is not very loud, but it has an ingenious technique for making its noise sound louder. The mole cricket makes a noise from inside a burrow. The shape of the burrow makes the mole cricket's noise louder. The sound can be around 110 decibels – as loud as a chainsaw!

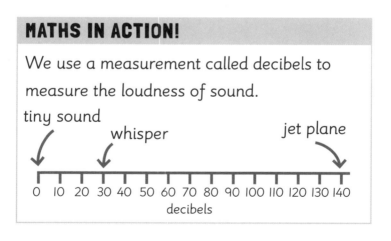

MATHS IN ACTION!

We use a measurement called decibels to measure the loudness of sound.

tiny sound

whisper

jet plane

0 10 20 30 40 50 60 70 80 90 100 110 120 130 140

decibels

Male mole crickets make a noise by hitting their wings together. Their forewings have teeth to help make the sound. The sound itself isn't very loud, but the burrow **amplifies** the noise.

Mole crickets have claws to help them dig.

The mole cricket's oval-shaped burrow is around 2.6 centimetres long. There is a horn-shaped opening which makes the noise sound louder.

The mole cricket sits in its burrow, between the bulb and the horn, when it "sings".

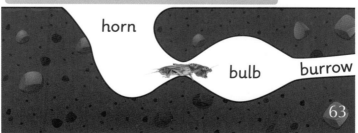

the mole cricket's "singing burrow"

horn

bulb

burrow

Fossils

Scientists have used cricket fossils to show that crickets have been making music for millions of years. The wings on the cricket fossils showed exactly how the crickets made their sound!

DID YOU KNOW?

Fossils are rocks that have preserved the remains of animals or plants that died millions of years ago. The first insects on Earth lived around 480 million years ago. Some of these early insects have been found in fossils.

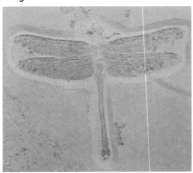

This is the fossil of a dragonfly.

MATHS IN ACTION!

Scientists have studied the fossil of a cricket that lived around 170 million years ago in the Jurassic period. The fossil showed the cricket's body very clearly — even the veins on its wings! The scientists used mathematics and magnifying glasses to help them build a model of the cricket. The model was so detailed that the scientists could make the model wings play the exact cricket song. This was the first time this song had been heard in millions of years!

Swarms

Locusts are a kind of grasshopper. They can be beige, black, green or yellow in colour. They travel in huge swarms, often eating all the plants from a large area in a matter of minutes. Because locusts destroy plants so quickly, people often talk about a **plague** of locusts.

Swarms are very noisy because a single swarm can contain millions or even billions of locusts!

MATHS IN ACTION!

Locusts have a unique way of avoiding colliding with each other. They have a movement detector which can work out the distance, direction and speed of locusts moving towards them. This allows them to avoid flying into other locusts in the swarm. Scientists want to use the locust's movement detector to help them design drones, robots and even self-driving cars. Locusts could help reduce road accidents!

Insects use maths in so many different ways, from their wing shapes and patterns to their dancing, flying and mating routines. Now some of the ideas we have learned about from insects are helping humans too! Scientists are using these ideas to create all kinds of things, from fire-extinguishers to self-driving cars.

Glossary

amplifies makes bigger

complex something with lots of parts

decibels a measure of sound volume

exoskeleton exterior skeleton – on the outside of the body

experiment a science test

honeycombs waxy structures built by bees in a hive

lenses see-through curved object that changes the way things look

mimic to copy something

mimicry when one animal copies another animal's appearance

parasite an animal or plant that lives in or on another animal or plant, and gets food from it

plague a sudden invasion of insects

predators animals that hunt other animals

prolegs fleshy limbs that are not true legs

repel to push back against with force

Index

About the author

How did you get into writing?

I always loved books as a child BUT
I wasn't very confident at reading
or spelling. My best subject at school
was maths! So, when I grew up, I did
a job that used lots of maths. I advised
people on how to save and invest
their money. One day, I decided to
be brave. I started to practise writing in my
spare time and grew in confidence. When I felt ready, I quit
my job to be a writer and I LOVE it!

Rachael Davis

What do you hope readers will get out of the book?

That maths, reading – and insects – are all very cool!
Sometimes maths can feel tricky to learn at school, but
when we look closely, we realise that we use maths all
the time in our everyday life, just like insects.

Is there anything in this book that relates to your own experiences?

I love the earwigs' origami-style wings because I enjoy doing
origami with my daughters.

Why did you want to write this book?

I enjoy discovering maths in the most unexpected places and
I wanted to share all the ingenious ways insects use maths.

What is it like for you to write?

I can be both shy and bubbly at times. I enjoy writing because I can do it on my own in a quiet space. Then, once my book is finished, I can read it to children on school visits and share it with my friends.

What is a book you remember loving reading when you were young?

My top picture book was *The Tiger Who Came to Tea* by Judith Kerr. I remember looking out my window hoping the tiger would come and visit me. I have no idea how many times my mum read it to me, but it must be at least a million! As I got a little older, I listened to a lot of audio books.

Which insect do you like best, and why?

I like butterflies the best, especially their beautiful symmetrical wings. Butterflies were my mum's top animal too.

What's your top example of maths in nature?

I love seeing all the spiral patterns in nature like on seashells, flowers, and snails. See if you can spot any spirals in nature next time you go outside!

How did you go about researching this book?

I read lots of books on insects as well as reports written by scientists who have studied insects.

Book chat

Which part of the book did you like best, and why?

What did you think of the book at the start? Did you change your mind as you read it?

If you had to give the book a new title, what would you choose?

Which do you think is the most interesting example of insect maths in the book?

What insect from the book would you most like to see and why?

Which part of the book surprised you most? Why?

Would you recommend this book to other people? If so, who?

If someone asked you what this book was about, what would you tell them?

Why do you think the book is called *Insect Maths*?

Did you know any of these insect facts before reading this book?

If you could ask the author one question, what would you ask?

What insect do you like best from the book?

Have you read any other books on insects?

Have you ever seen any of the insects in this book in real life?

Would you be interested in reading more books on insects?

Book challenge:
Draw your own insect with symmetrical wing patterns.

Collins
BIG CAT

Published by Collins
An imprint of HarperCollins*Publishers*
The News Building
1 London Bridge Street
London SE1 9GF
UK

Macken House
39/40 Mayor Street Upper
Dublin 1
D01 C9W8
Ireland

10 9 8 7 6

ISBN 978-0-00-862473-6

British Library Cataloguing-in-Publication Data
A catalogue record for this publication is available from the British Library.

Download the teaching notes and word cards to accompany this book at:
http://littlewandle.org.uk/signupfluency/

Get the latest Collins Big Cat news at
collins.co.uk/collinsbigcat

MIX
Paper | Supporting
responsible forestry
FSC
www.fsc.org
FSC™ C007454

Author: Rachael Davis
Illustrator: Andrew Pagram (Beehive illustration)
Publisher: Lizzie Catford
Product manager: Caroline Green
Series editor: Charlotte Raby
Commissioning editor: Suzannah Ditchburn
Development editor: Catherine Baker
Project manager: Emily Hooton
Content editor: Daniela Mora Chavarría
Copyeditor: Catherine Dakin
Phonics reviewer: Rachel Russ
Proofreader: Gaynor Spry
Picture researcher: Sophie Hartley
Cover designer: Sarah Finan
Typesetter: 2Hoots Publishing Services Ltd
Production controller: Katharine Willard

Collins would like to thank the teachers and children at the following schools who took part in the trialling of Big Cat for Little Wandle Fluency: Burley And Woodhead Church of England Primary School; Chesterton Primary School; Lady Margaret Primary School; Little Sutton Primary School; Parsloes Primary School.

Printed and bound in the UK

Acknowledgements
All rights reserved. No part of this publication may be reproduced, stored in a retrieval system, or transmitted in any form by any means, electronic, mechanical, photocopying, recording or otherwise, without the prior written permission of the Publisher or in the UK a license issued by the Copyright Licensing Agency Ltd.

Front cover: tl Tsekhmister/Shutterstock, tc Nature Picture Library/Alamy, tr Eric Isselee/Shutterstock, cr Lukas Gojda/Shutterstock, bl Keith J Smith/Alamy; back cover: tl & p3t Domiciano Pablo Romero Franco/Alamy, tr Peter Gudella/Shutterstock, bl tawin bunkoed/Shutterstock, br KPixMining/Alamy, p4b Eye of Science/Science Photo Library, p9t Nature Picture Library/Alamy, p9b Keith J Smith/Alamy, p16 Edwin Giesbers/Nature Picture Library, p21 Philippe Psaila/Science Photo Library, p23 Panther Media GmbH/Alamy, p29 Ted Kinsman/Science Photo Library, p33 David Parker/Science Photo Library, p35t Avalon.red/Alamy, p35b Oliver Wright/Nature Picture Library, p40t Westend61 GmbH/Alamy, p40b Andrew Darrington/Alamy, p42t Scott Camazine/Alamy, p42b Claus Lunau/Science Photo Library, p45l Chronicle/Alamy, p45r Kunstmuseum Basel Martin P. Bühler, p46tc Steven Iles/Alamy, p46br US Geological Survey/Science Photo Library, p48t Andrew Mackay/Alamy, p48b FLPA/Alamy, p49t FLPA/Alamy, p49b imageBROKER.com GmbH & Co. KG/Alamy, p50tl Photo © Derek Binns 35, p51br MYN/Lily Kumpe/Nature Picture Library, p54 blickwinkel/Alamy, p55tl Nature Production/Nature Picture Library, p55tr Dorling Kindersley ltd/Alamy, p57 yod67/Alamy, p61b blickwinkel/Alamy, p63 The Natural History Museum/Alamy, p64 BIOSPHOTO/Alamy, p65 blickwinkel/Alamy, p66 BILAL TARABEY/AFP/Getty, p70 Aaron Daniel Jacobsen. All other photos Shutterstock.